THE ANTITHESIS

THE ANTITHESIS

In The Image Of...

Tabu

Dedication

First, that their names may forever remain upon the minds of people of this world, I dedicate this book to my parents who were the perfect parents for me:

My mother, *Annie Ruth* gave me the space I needed to grow and evolve into the instrument the *Universe* intended to mold me into. I was in prison when she transcended; nevertheless, during her last visit she still had the love for me to say: "I am proud of the man you have become."

My father, *Royal Clyde,* whose quiet strength I inherited- taught me to be an effective father ... and accept that there are duties and sacrifices that define and separate the role from the individual.

My siblings: *Cynthia, Ronald,* and *Vincent* have always supported me in my dreams and ventures. With the success of this book, you will receive that starter kit we have always hoped one of us would be able to provide the others.

My son and my daughter who, when I returned from pen-state, invited me to share in their lives. You made coming home ... special. I have always wanted to have children that love me as much as I love them - and that is my greatest success.

Last, but not least, the aunts, uncles, nieces, cousins, neighbors, and countless members of my extended family who developed and defined my sense of community and what it means to be a member of a colloquy.

Thank You!

    Tabu

Table of Contents

In The Image Of ...

The Image 2
Confronting Truth 3
Biased 4
Foundations... 5
Reality... 6
Respond.. 7

In the Beginning

I Will Be ... ! 9

The Reading .... Genesis 1
The Creation Account.. 11

The Reading .... Genesis 2
"Formed" With A Purpose.. 14

The Reading .... Genesis 3
The Eden Account 17
Out of Eden 18

The Reading .... Genesis 4
The Pain of Shame 20
Two Adams... 21

Let There Be Light

The Creation Account 23
The Language 24
Godly Attributes 25
The Divine Separatist... 26

The Eden Account 29
"Formed" With A Purpose... 30
The "Vetting"... 31
The "Watchman".. 32
The "Dilemma".. 33
The Dispensation 34
An Encounter with Truth 35
An Enlightening Experience 36

The Transgression..37

"Emancipation".. 38

The Indictment.. 39

A Naked Shame 40

The Verdict..41

Out of Eden 42

Two Adams.. 43

The Imposition 44

"LIFE"..45

A Question of Paternity.. 46

Paramours..47

The Ruse

And ... Then 51

The Reading........................... Genesis 6

Favor 53

The Reading........................Genesis 7

The Digression 55

The Ordinance..56

The Beginning of the End

The Language 58

Immaculate Conception(s).. 60

A Walk with God 62

A Spiritual Conspiracy 63

Amicus Curiae 65

A Thirst for Blood.. 66

The Sorority..67

Reflections.. 69

Preface

We inherit lots of acts, traditions, and beliefs. Practices so ingrained within our fiber that personal sentiment creates an unexplainable hold and our "true selves" become fossilized for some future world to discover and only theorize about the way things were ... and/or could have been.

I was inspired to memorialize these summations because the spirit within me did more to dictate my path than I was able to do following socialized intentions for me.

Really, the choice was already made for me - much like the choice was already made for Jonah ... go figure. And if you believe in predestination, it has been decided for you as well.

Essentially, sometimes things become so compelling ... that our personal preservation and that of others relies upon the relinquishment of our own autonomy. So, we exercise *free will* and give over. It can be a bitter cup to drink from (Mat. 26:39).

If you are going to *put new wine into new bottles* (Mat. 9:17) there is a mandate to approach the truth unbeholden to any tradition, dogma, or agenda or you will only skew the experience.

From one perspective the sin we are born into could very well be that prison of flesh ... we are condemned to serve out that *life sentence* imposed upon us in the Garden. Remember, this book is about perspective.

Penning this portrait was not with the intent to guide, persuade, or direct you to any conclusions. What these passages speak to you are your conclusions. It is more of an opportunity to present in the best light what master crafters placed before an audience ... an audience called to dwell in a different realm and accept what was received as truth to the path of destiny.

This book is about you and asks that you address why you believe what you do and shine a shimmer of enlightenment upon the foundation of that belief – whether political, religious, etc.

This writing is a gift to you and attempts to address some of the many underlying questions some have regarding the scriptures; therefore, it is yours ... something to have for yourself.

IN THE IMAGE OF...

Tabu

The Image

Look at the Image of yourself in the Mirror.
Now, touch your right eye with your Right Hand.

THE ANTITHESIS

Confronting Truth

Is the Reflection an Exact Replica?
No!
The Reflection Touches the Left Eye with the Left Hand.

Biased

Everything ever spoken, written, or done has and will continue with a degree of "bias."

Even in the face of overwhelmingly convincing evidence to the contrary — socialization has conditioned us to rationalize and accept the most convenient resolution.

Bias must succumb to truth.

THE ANTITHESIS

Foundations

28:9 Whom shall he teach knowledge? And whom shall he make to understand doctrine?

Them that are weaned from the milk and drawn from the breasts.

28:10 For precept must be upon precept, precept upon precept; line upon line, line upon line: here a little, and there a little.

Isaiah (KJV)

Tabu

Reality

180° along the continuum lies
"The Antithesis"

THE ANTITHESIS

Respond

28:11 For with stammering lips and another tongue will he speak to this people.

28:13 ...that they might go, and fall backward, and be broken, and snared, and taken.

Isaiah (KJV)

IN THE BEGINNING

THE ANTITHESIS

I Will Be ...!

14:12   How art thou fallen from heaven, O Lucifer, son of the morning! How art thou cut down to the ground, which didst weaken the nations!

14:13   For thou hast said in thine heart, I will ascend into heaven, I will exalt my throne above the stars of God: I will sit also upon the mount of the congregation, in the sides of the north:

14:14   I will ascend above the heights of the clouds:
I will be like the Most High.

Isaiah (KJV)

The Reading

Genesis 1:

[1] In the beginning God created the heavens and the earth.

[2] The earth was formless and empty, and darkness covered the deep waters. And the Spirit of God was hovering over the surface of the waters.

[3] Then God said, "Let there be light," and there was light.

[4] And God saw that the light was good. Then **he separated the light from the darkness**. [5] *God called the light "day" and the darkness "night."*

And evening passed and morning came, marking the first day.

[6] Then God said, "let there be a space between the waters, to separate the waters of the heavens from the waters of the earth."

[7] And that is what happened. **God made this space to separate** the waters of the earth from the waters of the heavens. [8] God called the space "sky."

And evening passed and morning came, marking the second day.

[9] Then God said, "Let the waters beneath the sky flow together into one place, so dry ground may appear." And that is what happened. [10] God called the dry ground "land" and the waters "seas." And God saw that it was good. [11] Then God said, "Let the land sprout with vegetation — every sort of seed-bearing plant, and trees ... These seeds will then *produce the kinds of plants and trees from which they came*." And that is what happened.

[12] The land produced vegetation - all sorts of seed-bearing plants, and trees with seed-bearing fruit. Their seeds produced plants and trees of the same kind. And God saw that it was good.

[13] And evening passed and morning came, marking the third day.

THE ANTITHESIS

The Creation Account

¹⁴ Then God said, "Let great lights appear in the sky to **separate the day from the night.** Let them mark off the seasons, days, and years. ¹⁵ Let these lights in the sky shine down on the earth." And that is what happened.

¹⁶ *God made two great lights, the sun and the moon* - the larger one to govern the day, and the smaller one to govern the night. He also made the stars. ¹⁷ God set these lights in the sky to light the earth, ¹⁸ to govern the day and night, and to **separate the light from the darkness**. And God saw it was good.

¹⁹ And evening passed and morning came, marking the fourth day.

²⁰ Then God said, "Let the waters swarm with fish and other life. Let the skies be filled with birds of every kind." ²¹ So God created great sea creatures and every living thing that scurries and swarms in the water, and every sort of bird - each producing offspring of the same kind. And God saw that it was good.

²² Then God blessed them saying, "**Be fruitful and multiply.** Let the fish fill the seas, and let the birds multiply on the earth."

²³ And evening passed and morning came, marking the fifth day.

²⁴ Then God said, "Let the earth produce every sort of animal, each *producing offspring of the same kind* — livestock, small animals that scurry along the ground, and wild animals." And that is what happened. ²⁵ God made all sort of wild animals, livestock, and small animals, each able to produce offspring of the same kind. And God saw that it was good.

²⁶ Then God said, "<u>Let us make human beings</u> ***in our image***, to be like ourselves. They will reign over the fish in the sea, the birds in the sky, the livestock, all the wild animals on the earth, and the small animals that scurry along the ground."

²⁷ So <u>God created human beings</u> ***in his own image***. In the image of God he created them; male and female he created them.

²⁸ Then God blessed them and said, ***"Be fruitful and multiply***. Fill the earth and govern it. Reign over the fish in the sea, the birds in the sky, and all the animals that scurry along the ground."

²⁹ Then God said, Look! <u>I have given you</u> every seed-bearing plant throughout the earth and <u>all the fruit trees for your food</u>.

³⁰ And I have given every green plant as food for all the wild animals, the birds in the sky, and the small animals that scurry along the ground — everything that has life." And that is what happened.

³¹ Then God looked over all he had made, and he saw that it was very good!

And evening passed and morning came, <u>marking the sixth day</u>.

THE ANTITHESIS

The Reading

Genesis 2:

[1] _So the creation of the heavens and the earth and everything in them was completed._ [2] On the seventh day God had finished his work of creation, so he rested from all his work. [3] And God blessed the seventh day and declared it holy, because it was the day when he rested from all his work of creation.

[4] **This is the account of the creation of the heavens and the earth.**

"Formed" With A Purpose

When the L ORD God made the earth and the heavens, ⁵ neither wild plants nor grains were growing on the earth. The L ORD God had not yet sent rain to water the earth, and **there were no people to cultivate the soil.** ⁶ Instead, springs came up from the ground and watered all the land.

⁷Then the **L ORD God "formed"** _the man from the dust of the ground._ He breathed the breath of life into the man's nostrils, and man became a living person.

⁸ Then the L ORD God planted a garden in Eden in the east, and there he placed the man he had made.

⁹ The L ORD God made all sorts of trees grow up from the ground — trees that were beautiful and that produce delicious fruit. In the middle of the garden he placed **the tree of life** and **the tree of the knowledge of good and evil.**

---

¹⁵ The L ORD **God placed the man in the Garden of Eden to tend and watch over it.** ¹⁶ But the L ORD God warned him, _"You may freely eat the fruit of every tree_ in the garden — ¹⁷ except _the tree of the knowledge of good and evil._ If you eat its fruit, you are sure to die.

¹⁸ Then the L ORD God said, ***"It is not good for man to be alone.*** I will make him a helper who is just right for him."

¹⁹ So the **L ORD God "formed"** from the ground all the wild animals and all the birds of the sky. He brought them to the man to see what he would call them, and the man chose a name for each one. ²⁰ He gave names to all the livestock, all the birds of the sky, and all the wild animals. But still there was no helper just right for him.

THE ANTITHESIS

21 So the LORD God caused the man to fall into a deep sleep. While the man slept, the LORD God took out one of the man's ribs and closed up the opening. 22 The LORD God made a woman from the rib, and he brought her to the man.

23 "At last!" the man exclaimed. "This one is bone from my bone, and flesh from my flesh! She will be called **'woman,'** because she was taken from the 'man.'"

24 This explains why a man leaves his father and mother and is joined with his wife, and the two are united into one.

25 Now the man and his wife were both naked, but they felt no shame.

Tabu

The Reading

Genesis 3:

¹ The serpent was the shrewdest of all the wild animals the LORD God **had made**. One day he asked the woman, *"Did God really say you must not eat the fruit* from any of the trees in the garden?

² "Of course we may eat fruit from the trees in the garden," the woman replied. ³ "It's only the fruit from the tree in the middle of the garden that we are not allowed to eat. God said, 'You must not eat it or even touch it; if you do, you will die."

⁴ "You won't die!" the serpent replied to the woman." ⁵ "God knows that your eyes will be opened as soon as you eat it, and you will be like God, knowing both good and evil."

⁶ The woman was convinced. She saw that the tree was beautiful and its fruit looked delicious, and she wanted the wisdom it would give her. So, she took some of the fruit and ate it.

Then she gave some to her husband, who was with her, and he ate it, too. ⁷ At that moment their eyes were opened, and they suddenly felt shame at their nakedness. So, they sewed fig leaves together to cover themselves.

⁸ When the cool evening breezes were blowing, the man and his wife heard the LORD God walking about in the garden. So, they hid from the LORD God among the trees. ⁹ Then the LORD God called to the man, "Where are you?"

¹⁰ He replied, "I heard you walking in the garden, so I hid. I was afraid because I was naked."

¹¹ "Who told you that you were naked?" the LORD God asked.

16

THE ANTITHESIS

The Eden Account

"Have you eaten from the tree whose fruit I commanded <u>you</u> not to eat?"

¹² The man replied, "It was **the woman you gave me** who gave me the fruit, and I ate it."

¹³ Then the LORD God asked the woman, "What have you done?" "The serpent deceived me," she replied. "That's why I ate it."

¹⁴ Then the LORD God said to the serpent, "Because you have done this, <u>you are cursed more than all animals</u>, domestic, and wild. You will crawl on your belly, groveling in the dust as long as you live.

¹⁵ And I will cause hostility between you and the woman, and between **your offspring** and **her offspring**. He will strike your head and you will strike his heel."

¹⁶ Then he said to the woman, "I will sharpen the pain of your pregnancy, and in pain you will give birth. And *you will desire to control your husband* but he will rule over you."

¹⁷ And to the man he said, "Since you listened to your wife and ate from the tree whose *fruit I commanded you not to eat*, the ground is cursed because of you. All your life you will struggle to scratch a living from it."

¹⁸ It will grow thorns and thistles for you, though you will eat of its grains. ¹⁹ By the sweat of your brow will you have food to eat **until you return to the ground from which you were made.** For you were made from dust, and to dust you will return."

Out of Eden

²⁰ Then the man— **Adam— named his wife Eve,** because she would become the <u>mother of all who live</u>. ²¹ And the Lord God made clothing from animal skins for Adam and his wife.

²² Then the LORD God said, "Look, ***the man*** has become like us, knowing both good and evil. What if they reach out, take fruit from the tree of life and eat it? Then they will live forever!"

²³ So the LORD God banished them from the Garden of Eden, and he sent Adam out to cultivate the ground from which he had been made. ²⁴ After sending them out, the LORD God stationed mighty cherubim to the east of the Garden of Eden. And he placed a flaming sword that flashed back and forth to guard the way to the tree of life.

THE ANTITHESIS

The Reading

Genesis 4:

¹ Now **Adam had sexual relations with his wife,** Eve, and she became pregnant. When she gave birth to Cain, she said, "With the LORD's help, <u>I have produced a man!</u>" ² Later she gave birth to his brother and named him Abel.

When they grew up, Abel became a shepherd, while Cain cultivated the ground. ³ When it was time for the harvest, Cain presented some of his crops as a gift to the LORD. ⁴ Abel also brought a gift - the best of the firstborn lambs from his flock. The LORD accepted Abel and his gift, ⁵ but he did not accept Cain and his gift. This made Cain very angry, and he looked dejected.

⁶ "Why are you so angry?" the LORD God asked Cain. "Why do you look so dejected?" ⁷ You will be accepted if you do what is right. But if you refuse to do what is right, then watch out! Sin is crouching at the door, eager to control. But you must subdue it and be its master."

⁸ One day Cain suggested to his brother, "Let's go out into the fields." And while they were in the field, Cain attacked his brother, Abel, and killed him.

The Pain of Shame

⁹ Afterward the LORD asked Cain, "Where is your brother? Where is Abel?" "I don't know," Cain responded. "Am I my brother's guardian?"

¹⁰ But the LORD said, "What have you done? Listen! Your brother's blood cries out to me from the ground!

¹¹ <u>Now you are cursed</u> and banished from the ground, which has swallowed your brother's blood.

¹² <u>No longer will the ground yield good crops for you</u>, no matter how hard you work! From now on you will be a homeless wanderer on the earth."

¹³ Cain replied to the LORD, "My punishment is too great for me to bear! ¹⁴ You have banished me from the land and from your presence; you have made me a homeless wanderer. Anyone who finds me will kill me!"

¹⁵ The LORD replied, "No, for I will give a sevenfold punishment to anyone who kills you." Then the **LORD put a mark on Cain** to warn anyone who might kill him. ¹⁶ So Cain left the LORD's presence and settled in the land of Nod, **east of Eden.**

THE ANTITHESIS

Two Adams

²⁵ **Adam had sexual relations with his wife again,** and she gave birth to another son. **She named him Seth**, for she said, "God has granted me another son in place of Abel, whom Cain killed." ²⁶ When Seth grew up, he had a son and named him Enosh. At that time people first began to _worship the LORD by name._

Genesis 5:

¹ This is the written account of the descendants of Adam. When God created _human beings,_ he made them to be like himself. ² _He created them male and female,_ and he blessed them and called them "_human._"

³ When Adam was 130 years old, he became father of a son who was just like him - in his very image. **He named his son Seth**. ⁴ After the birth of Seth, Adam lived another 800 years, and he had other sons and daughters. ⁵ **Adam live 930 years**, and **then he died.**

LET THERE BE LIGHT

The Creation Account

[1] In the beginning God created the heavens and the earth. [2] The earth was formless and empty, and darkness covered the deep waters. And the Spirit of God was hovering over the surface of the waters.

The textual footnote of the *Tyndale* New Living Translation states Genesis 1:1 begins as such: "In the beginning when God created the heavens and the earth..." - or - "When God began to create the heavens and the earth..."

Either way is sufficient for this contemplation because, as it is, verse 1 addresses the creation saga in the past tense as if it was a foregone conclusion, which leaves the subsequent verses to detail the means to that end.

Nevertheless, we must first consider the state of things before the creation saga began. Thus, the wording "When God began to create the heavens and the earth..." is more appropriate for referencing the condition of that pre-existent material of *formless and empty* cosmic mass hidden beneath the *dark depths* of the waters, which later revealed i.e., earth.

[6]... "Let there be a space between the waters, to separate the waters of the heavens from the waters of earth." [7] And that is what happened. **God made this space to separate** the waters of the earth from the waters of the heavens. [8] God called the space "sky."

And evening passed and morning came, <u>marking the second day.</u>

The Language

Thus, with the parting of the waters on day two, the process of creation actually began; and on day three of creation:

> 9 Then God said, "let the waters beneath of the sky flow together into one place, so dry ground may appear." And that is what happened. 10 God called the dry ground "land" and the waters "seas." And God saw that it was good.

Wherefore with the corralling of the waters beneath the sky, dry land appeared, and earth was not created but realized. *As we can so vividly recall in Gen.1:1 ~ The earth was [already there] formless and empty...Then God said, "Let there be light..." Then he separated the light from the darkness. So, the creation of light <u>not</u> the earth was the first order of the day on God's agenda.*

Gen. 1:6 - 8 of the King James Version, the "space" **God made** *is referred to as the firmament (Heaven)...marking the second day.*

So, the scriptures give room to the posturing of scientists who declare the *physical* earth pre-dates the Biblical account of the event that created earth in name and as a result of an act of transformation.

This position must be expounded upon, not as an attempt to call into question the creation account, but as a backdrop to the preface's appreciation for the nuances of the language, its crafting to communicate a purpose, and our construing and perceiving of it and... thus, the scriptures.

THE ANTITHESIS

Godly Attributes

Be it as it may, in the beginning "the earth" was formless, empty, and dark. Then on the first day of creation God uttered those eventful words that set the creation chain-of-events into motion:

> 3 Then God said, "Let there be light," and there was light. 4 And God saw that <u>the light was good</u>. ***Then he separated the light from the darkness.*** 5 God called the light "day" and the darkness "night."

From this point, when we view the language of the scripture, we are forced to not just witness the linguistic overtones, but also to consider the *thematic* expressions therein.

As such, the first themes we notice also ascribe a particular set of attributes to the God of Genesis 1. Out of the abundance of caution and respect to the various schools of thought, I say, because <u>God is such a generic term</u> and we are particularly concerned with contemplating descriptive attributes that contribute to our understanding of Him, please, allow me to address His eminence by His first ascribed attribute - that is- as the "Creator."

Additionally, for purposes of this observation then we will point out the acts ascribing His second attribute for contemplation is that of a separatist (not in the secular connotation, but void of any racial, cultural, or ethnic favoring) - for *separatism (sanctification)* reigns high within this theological rhetoric.

The Divine Separatist

When the "Creator" pronounced those eventful words "Let there be light," for many that means that on the first day of creation He created the sun that produced this *light* as it is referred to. However, that is not scripturally sound for neither the sun nor the moon was created until the fourth day of creation.

> [14] Then God said, "Let great lights appear in the sky **to separate** the day from the night. Let them mark off the seasons, days, and years. [15] Let these lights in the sky shine down on the earth." and that is what happened. [16] **God made two great lights**, the sun and the moon - the larger one to govern the day, and the smaller one to govern the night. He also made the stars. [17] God set these lights in the sky to light the earth, [18] to govern the day and night, and **to separate** *the light from the darkness*. And God saw that it was good.
>
> [19] And evening passed and morning came, marking the fourth day.

Let us examine the purpose of these two great lights with respect to the language of versus 14 - 19. First let us agree that these two great lights, the sun and the moon, were designated to shine down on the earth and function as *time markers*: "Let them mark off the seasons, days, and years."

Then, let us agree to, even possibly, disagree that before that first pronouncement "Let there be light" *earth* was formless and empty, and darkness covered the deep waters; therefore, earth *existed before the beginning of time*, which was not birthed until day four of creation.

THE ANTITHESIS

So, neither day one; nor day two; day three; or any of those days with regards to the creation account constitute a twenty-four-hour day for prior <u>acts</u> of the "Creator."

So, since the first act of the "Creator" was to *separate* the light from the darkness, then, what must we purport this *light* to be manifested on i.e., day one was Knowledge (e.g., a plan).

While it would be quite simple to declare this "knowledge" to be a mere shared consensus in the planning stages regarding what to do with this formless and empty piece of cosmic rubble we know as earth, but this act of separating the light from the darkness goes beyond that understanding.

Knowledge in this case can be fittingly defined as gnosis, which is that *intuitive* apprehension of spiritual truths; that which is beyond intellectual intelligence or rationalized knowledge. Thus, with knowledge being the "light" (day) then circumstance demands ignorance to be the "darkness" (night). In keeping with the creation theme of sanctification...then the Creator intended for this *esoteric* knowledge to be segregated from mundane ignorance. This knowledge embodied the mind of the "Creator" and His *ulterior motive* for creation.

When the "Creator" *separated* the waters of the heavens from the waters of the earth, He called the space sky (the consequential result of the act of separating). When He separated the waters beneath the sky, dry land appeared (the consequential result of the act of separating); thus, dry land was the effect "realized" not created. When He separated the great lights of the sky, He made the stars. On each occasion when He separated elements a natural phenomenon filled the space between the two extremes. FYI: The moon does not produce its own light; it reflects light from the sun.

Only on a few occasions during the creation process were elements separated and the "Creator" did not place something there to fill the resulting *void* (emptiness). One of those occasions was on Day One when He separated the light from the darkness; He never filled that void. The next memorable occasion when the "Creator" separated an element of His own doing was when He *separated* the (wo)man from man.

Thus, we have two *voids* that need to be filled: (1) the void brought into effect by the *separation* of the light from the darkness manifested on Day One of creation and (2) the void brought into effect by the *separation* of the (wo)man from the man who was formed from the dust of the ground.

This leaves us with an interesting dilemma. How did the "Creator" intend to protect (govern) this celestial knowledge ("light") from the influence of common mundane ignorance ("darkness")? Answer: *God made two great lights...the larger one **to govern** the day, and the smaller one **to govern** the night."* The informed will govern the ill-informed.

———————————————————

Creation was completed by Genesis 2 verse 4 and purportedly, everyone was created equal:

> [1] So the creation of the heavens and the earth and
> everything in them was completed. [2] On the seventh day
> God had finished his work of creation, so he rested from all
> his work. [3] And God blessed the seventh day and declared it
> holy, because it was the day when he rested from all his
> work of creation.
>
> [4] **This is the account of the creation of the heavens
> and the earth.**

The Eden Account

At the end of the creation account, what the "Creator" spoke in the spiritual realm manifested on the earth: On Day Three of creation, it was pronounced "Let the land sprout with vegetation." And that is what happened. On Day Five of creation, it was pronounced "Let the skies be filled with birds of every kind." And that is what happened. On Day Six of creation, it was pronounced "Let the earth produce every sort of animal each *producing offspring of the same kind* - livestock, small animals that scurry along the ground, and wild animals." And that is what happened.

However, with the giving of dominion to the human beings created in His image, clearly, He could not see Himself as a laborer of the land:

> When the LORD God made the earth and the heavens,
> 5 neither wild plants nor grains were growing on the earth.
> The LORD God had not yet sent rain to water the earth, and
> **there were no people to cultivate the soil.**
>
> Genesis 2

Thus, to manifest this spiritual dispensation within the secular landscape, the *Creator* "formed" a man from the dust of the ground for that purpose - to cultivate the soil that is.

> 7 Then the **LORD God "formed"** *the man from the dust of the ground*. He breathed the breath of life into the man's nostrils, and man became a living person.
>
> 8 Then the LORD God planted a garden in Eden in the east, and there he placed the man he had made.

"Formed" With A Purpose

Notice the language used when the *Creator* "formed" man (Adam) from the dust of the ground.

First, He never pronounced this "formed" man to be good. Secondly, this "formed" man (Adam) was not "formed" from the soil within the Garden but only later placed there. Hold that thought!

> [15] Then LORD **God placed the man in the Garden of Eden to tend and watch over it.**

So, from his inception "formed" man (Adam) was given to husbandry - cultivation of the land.

Now we are not given any recognizable hints as to how long "formed" man (Adam) cultivated the soil from which he was "formed" before he was placed in the Garden of Eden; however, there are two points of interest that must be addressed that will unravel as we continue along this line of discourse: (1) the "Creator" never commanded "formed" man (Adam) to be fruitful and multiply (for he had no mate that was just right for him) and (2) we will come to understand that the "Creator" set forth an atmosphere to keep His "formed" entity on a separate playing field from His "created" entities.

So, armed with his innate mundane knowledge (darkness) of the soil as of himself, "formed" man (Adam) is placed in the Garden of Eden with only one prohibition:

[16] *"You may freely eat the fruit of every tree* in the garden - [17]*except the tree of the knowledge of good and evil.* **If you eat its fruit, you are sure to die.**

THE ANTITHESIS

The "Vetting"

Never having pronounced "formed" man (Adam) *to be good* the "Creator" reinforced His warning, thereby, further displaying His distrust for "formed" man (Adam):

> [18]Then the LORD God said, "***It is not good for man to be alone***. I will make him a helper who is just right for him."

Soon to be revealed, the "Creator" was not speaking of a *helper* in the context of a compatible companion, but as an accountability partner - a "watcher," someone or something that the "Creator" could rest assure would discourage "formed" man (Adam) from acquiring the knowledge of good and evil.

> [19]So the **LORD God "formed"** from the ground all the **wild animals** and all the **birds of the sky.**

Remember, on Day Five of creation He had already created all the birds of the sky; likewise, on Day Six of creation He had already created all kinds of domestic and wild animals.

So, it is safe to conclude the "Creator" presumed one of "formed" man (Adam's) own kind - formed from the ground - would be the perfect choice.

> He brought them to the man to see what he would call them, and the man chose a name for each one. [20]He gave names to the livestock, all the birds in the sky, and all the wild animals. **But still there was no helper just right for him.**

The "Watchman"

The "formed" man was not much like Him—this man was "formed" from the dust of the ground. So, the "Creator" resolved to divide the house of Adam with one not "created" in His image, but empathetic to His purpose.

> 21So the LORD God caused the ["formed"] man to fall into a deep sleep. While the ["formed"] man slept, the LORD God took out one of the "formed" man's ribs [God separated and "formed" (wo)man from the "formed" male] and closed up the opening.

Wherefore, the use of an empathizer is not a practice conceived only in the minds of men but is a demonstration resulting from a spiritual dispensation being manifested within the secular landscape.

In Ezekiel 33, when Ezekiel was appointed as the "watchman" of Israel, these words went forth:

2" Son of man, give your people this message: "When I bring an army against a country, **the people of that land choose one of their own to be a watchman.**

3When the watchman sees the enemy coming, he sounds the alarm to warn the people. 4Then if those who hear the alarm refuse to take action, **it is their own fault if they die**. 5They heard the alarm but ignored it, so the responsibility is theirs. If they had listened to the warning, they could have saved their lives.

6But **if the watchman sees the enemy coming and doesn't sound the alarm to warn the people**, he is responsible for their captivity. They will die in their sins, but **I will hold the watchman responsible for their deaths.**"

THE ANTITHESIS

The "Dilemma"

²² The LORD God made a woman from the rib, and he brought her to the man. ²³ "At last!" the man exclaimed. "This one is bone from my bone, and flesh from my flesh!"

She will be called 'woman,' because she was taken from 'man.'" ²⁴This explains why *a man leaves his father and his mother* and is joined to his wife, and the two are united into one.

²⁵*Now the man and his wife were both naked, but they felt no shame.*

"Formed" Adam had neither father nor mother. Therefore, unless "formed" Adam regarded the "created" woman and the "created" Adam as his mother and father, the foundation of this parental concept escapes this author.

Yet, the *Creator* never pronounced "them" to be "good." Nevertheless, even without that pronouncement, the man and his wife were "naked" ... and they felt no "shame."

The Dispensation

Thus, with the act of separating the (wo)man from the "formed" man (Adam) the "Creator" provided Himself with a "watchman" to ensure protection of His celestial knowledge (light) from being apprehended by the man He "formed" from the dust of the ground.

For we must recall, even after the "Creator" separated the (wo)man from the "formed" man (Adam), He never gave them the command to "*be fruitful and multiply,*" and **the earth ... subdue it**.

The proclamation of Genesis 1:28 was never explicitly bestowed upon "formed" man (Adam) and the woman who was *made* from him.

Because "formed" man and his woman were not clothed with this authority of government they were *naked* (broke), but they felt no shame.

THE ANTITHESIS

An Encounter with Truth

In Genesis 3, we are introduced to the *serpent*, a title that proves to be a mere epithet assigned to him due to the resulting effect of his shrewdness.

On the contrary, for this discussion, we refer to the *serpent* as the *"Revealer"* for this attribute is rightfully placed.

> [1]The serpent was the shrewdest of the all the wild animals the Lord God had made. One day he asked the woman, *"Did God really say* <u>you</u> *must not eat the fruit* from any of the trees in the garden?"
>
> [2]"Of course <u>we</u> may eat fruit from the trees in the garden," the woman replied. [3]"It's only the fruit from the tree in the middle of the garden that <u>we</u> are not allowed to eat. God said, 'You must not eat it or even touch it; if you do, you will die.'"

In this dialogue when the "Revealer" asked the (wo)man, *"Did God really say* **you** *must not eat the fruit* from any of the trees in the garden?" This question was directed <u>specifically</u> to her (i.e., second-person singular) and was not intended in the plural (you all) sense.

Yet the effect of this direct question shows us that the (wo)man understood the exchange to require a response in the first-person plural - *"we"* - <u>are not allowed to eat</u>.

This warning was given to "formed" man (Adam) only; never was the (wo)man prohibited to eat from the tree of the knowledge of good and evil.

An Enlightening Experience

With the appointment of the (wo)man to act as a "watchman" over the "formed" man (Adam) in the Garden that marked the *Creator's* attempt to fill that *void* manifested by the *separation* of the light from the darkness during Day-One of Creation.

Now without that *void* being filled that was brought into effect by the separation of the man and the (wo)man, the "Revealer" sets out to correct that condition that manifested itself as the (wo)man's ignorance.

> 4 "You won't die!" the ["**_Revealer_**"] replied to the woman." 5 "[The "Creator"] knows that your eyes will be opened **as soon as** you eat it, and you will be like [The "Creator"], knowing both good and evil."

When (wo)man was *separated* from "*formed*" man (Adam) she shared a divine reality of purpose with the *Creator* and the knowledge of good and evil would become the (wo)man's delayed inheritance and crimson legacy.

(Wo)man just needed to be reassured of what she inherently knew inside of her *unconscious mind*...the "Revealer" was not misleading her. The (wo)man, desirous to be enlightened, was easily convinced:

> 6 ...she wanted the wisdom it would give her. So, she took some of the fruit and ate it.

At that moment, when the (wo)man ate the fruit from the *tree of the knowledge of good and evil*, nothing happened; no shame came over her because possession of this celestial knowledge was (wo)man's intended state of consciousness.

THE ANTITHESIS

The Transgression

But then, (wo)man violated the duty of her station:

> Then she gave some to her husband, who was with her, and
> he ate it too. 7At that moment their eyes were opened, and
> they suddenly felt shame at their nakedness. So, they
> sewed fig leaves together to cover themselves.

Prior to Genesis 3:21 neither did "created" man (Adam), (wo)man, nor "formed" man (Adam) have a fleshy covering over their bodies as traditionally viewed - so the nakedness for which they were ashamed cannot be understood as their genitalia were exposed and they desired to cover themselves.

There was no evil in existence — only that which was judged to be "good" and that which was not. So, we must understand whatever the "*Creator*" failed to judge as "good" was to be understood as "evil."

The "*Creator*" saw that *the light was good,* and He separated it from the darkness. Darkness was an attribute of the earth in its pre-existent state (condition) and when this man (Adam) was "formed" from the dust of the ground, he possessed the attributes of that from which he was formed.

When the land sprouted with vegetation - all sort of seed-bearing plants and trees with seed-bearing fruit...the "Creator" saw that *it was good.*

But when the "*Creator*" formed the man from the dust of the ground and when He *separated* (wo)man from "formed" man (Adam), the "*Creator*" never declared either act to be good. So, by way of implication, we must conclude they **covered themselves with fig leaves to give themselves the "appearance" of being good.**

"Emancipation"

The Prophet Isaiah said *it is your sins that separate you from God* (Isa. 59:2).

> [8]When the cool evening breezes were blowing, the man and his wife heard the LORD God walking about in the garden. So, they hid from the LORD God among the trees. [9]Then the LORD God called to the man, "Where are you?"

> [10]He replied, "I heard you walking in the garden, so I hid. I was afraid because I was naked."

> [11]**"Who told you** that you were naked?" the LORD God asked. "Have you eaten from the tree whose fruit I commanded you not to eat?"

Because the *"Creator"* never denied to "formed" man (Adam) that he was naked the *Creator's* inquiry was premised upon whether "formed" man (Adam) believed because he was "told" he was naked or did he come to this realization on his own accord via disobedience. Wherefore:

> [12]The man replied, "It was the woman you gave me who gave me the fruit, and I ate it."

THE ANTITHESIS

The Indictment

The human beings (male and female) that were *"created"* in the image of the *"Creator"* were intended to be immortal and to govern the earth.

> 1:29... "Look! I have given you every seed-bearing plant throughout the earth and **all the fruit trees for your food.**"

While the man (Adam) who was "formed" from the dust of the ground was meant to cultivate the soil.

> 2:5...**there were no people to cultivate the soil**... 7Then the **LORD God "formed"** <u>the man</u> *from the dust of the ground*... 8 Then the LORD God planted a garden in Eden in the east, and <u>there he placed the man</u> he had made.

What we have here is truth that we must, first, admit to ourselves. The "serpent" (i.e., the *Revealer*) neither lied nor deceived the (wo)man and "formed" man (Adam) was the only actor who *disobeyed* a direct warning.

When the "Revealer," enlightened the (wo)man no transgression was cognizable...disobedience was yet to occur. Only when the (wo)man permitted "formed" man to partake of the fruit from the *tree of the knowledge of good and evil* did they become conscious (*self-conscious*) of their transgressions.

Obviously, "formed" man (Adam) disobeyed the commandment <u>not</u> to eat from the tree of the *knowledge* of good and evil.

2:16 But the LORD God warned him, *"You may freely eat the fruit of every tree* in the garden - 17 <u>except</u> *the tree of the knowledge of good and evil. If* **you eat its fruit you are sure to die."**

A Naked Shame

"Formed" man could not blame the (wo)man because he was not ignorant to what the *Creator* said to him!

> 3:17 "Since you listened to your wife and ate from the tree whose fruit I commanded you not to eat, **the ground** is cursed because of you."

On the other hand, since the *Creator* never commanded the (wo)man not to eat the fruit of the tree of the knowledge of good and evil her **acquiring of this knowledge** <u>was a non-issue</u>.

> 3:13 Then the LORD God asked the woman, "What have you done?" "The serpent deceived me," she replied. "That's why I ate it."

The (wo)man's sin was not eating the fruit of the tree of the knowledge of good and evil. Remember when the "*Revealer*" enlightened the (wo)man and she partook of the fruit nothing out of the ordinary occurred.

> "God winked at [her] ignorance..."
>
> Acts 17:30

Thus, the incorrigible sin was the sharing of the forbidden fruit (esoteric *celestial knowledge*) with the mundane - "formed" man (Adam)? The watchman had failed.

> 6But *if the watchman sees the enemy coming and doesn't sound the alarm to warn the people,* he is responsible for their captivity. They will die in their sins, but *I will hold the watchman responsible for their deaths."*
>
> Ezekiel 33

THE ANTITHESIS

The Verdict

The (wo)man was <u>guilty of the act of commission</u>. For after she had eaten the fruit of the tree of the knowledge of good and evil, she became an enlightened being; she was like the *Creator*. Nevertheless, now knowing better … sharing the reality of mind with the *Creator*, (wo)man gave this forbidden fruit to "formed" man (Adam).

> 3:14Then the Lord God said to the serpent, "Because you have done this, <u>you are cursed more than all animals</u>, domestic, and wild.

"Formed" man (Adam) was <u>guilty in the first-degree</u> of direct disobedience to the "*Creator*" by becoming as He is – having knowledge of both good and evil.

But hold on, why was the serpent punished?! He derailed the *Creator's* plan. He enlightened the (wo)man without warning her of the consequences attached to being reckless with esoteric knowledge…

Furthermore, we must understand the "serpent" to be an epithet … not to be a reptilian but "created" man (Adam). Thus, the "serpent" (*Revealer / Adam*) was <u>guilty of the act of omission</u>. For he, having (wo)man's attention, did not prevent her from sharing this sacred fruit with "formed" man (Adam).

Just for fun, could the "serpent" have wanted the (wo)man for himself and he planned to use the (wo)man to get "formed" man out of the way. But did the results work to his detriment?

Out of Eden

3:22 Then the LORD God said, "Look, **the man has become like us,** knowing both good and evil. What if they reach out, take fruit from the tree of life and eat it? Then they will live forever!"

3:24 After sending them out, the LORD God stationed mighty cherubim to the east of the Garden of Eden. And He placed a flaming sword that flashed back and forth to guard the way to the tree of life.

THE ANTITHESIS

Two Adams

Perplexing; yet, interesting. When you search the *Young's Analytical Concordance to the Bible* for the etymology of "Adam," you will discover the entry "*of the ground.*" Comparatively, when the same referenced material is used for the etymology of "man," you will discover the entry "human being" (i.e., Adam). Additionally, you will find references to verses regarding "created" man who reflects the image of God (the *Creator*) and "formed" man whose connection is with the earth (the dust of the ground).

As artfully crafted as the language may be, defining markers are dispersed. On the Sixth Day of creation, the "*Creator*" made these comments:

> 1:26 Then God said, "**Let us make human beings** in our image, **to be like ourselves…**"

> 1:27 So God created human beings in His own image. In the image of God, He created them; <u>male and female</u> He created them (plural).

> 1:28 Then **God blessed them** and said, **"Be fruitful and multiply."**

As we enter Genesis 2, verse four clearly demonstrates that all "God" was going to create had been created: 2:4 "*This is the account of the creation of the heavens and earth.*" Then our divining rod encounters these words:

2:7 Then the LORD God **"formed" the man from the dust of the ground.** He breathed the breath of life into the man's nostrils, and <u>man became a living person</u> (singular).

As such, it is necessary to refer to one "Adam" as created "man" and the other "Adam" as "formed man."

The Imposition

3:23 So the LORD God banished them from the Garden of Eden, and *He sent Adam out to cultivate the ground from which he had been made.*

Momentarily, let us look back at the imposition of each one's punishment.

The Serpent / Revealer / "Created" man (Adam)

3:15 You will crawl on your belly, groveling in the dust as long as you live. And I will cause hostility between you and the woman, and *between your offspring and her offspring.* He will strike your head and you will strike his heel."

Question: What was to cause enmity between the Revealer and the (wo)man?

(Wo)man / Eve

3:16 Then He said to the woman, "I will sharpen the pain of your pregnancy, and *in pain you will give birth.* And you will desire to control your husband, but he will rule over you."

Since Genesis 1:28 the female had been commanded to be fruitful and multiply; however, this declaration was never bestowed upon the (wo)man made from "formed" Adam. Therefore, she would never share this experience with "formed" man.

"Formed" man (Adam)

3:17 "...[T]he ground is cursed because of you. All your life you will struggle to scratch a living from it. 18 It will grow thorns and thistles for you, though you will eat of its grains. 19 By the sweat of your brow will you have food to eat *until you return to the ground from which you were made.* For you were made from dust, and to dust will you return."

THE ANTITHESIS

"LIFE"

3:21 And the LORD God made clothing from animal skins for Adam and his wife.

Imprisoned in clothing made from animal skins "they" were expelled from the Garden of Eden to carry out their divine punishment and (Wo)man / Eve becomes the paramour for the "two Adams."

Lest we forget, during the divine separation, while "formed" man (Adam) slept:

> 2:21 ...the LORD God took out one of the man's ribs and closed up the opening. 22 Then the LORD God made a woman from the rib, and He brought her to the man. 23 "At last!" the man exclaimed. "This one is bone from my bone, and flesh from my flesh! **She will be called 'woman,'** because she was taken from 'man.'"

Yet, after the great sin was committed and expulsion from the Garden of Eden occurred, "formed" man (Adam) named the (wo)man Eve and declared her to be his wife.

> 3:20 Then the man - Adam—named his wife Eve[1], because she would be the <u>mother of all who live</u>."

Genesis 4:1 states *"Now Adam had sexual relations with his wife, Eve..."*

We know this birth produced twins - Cain and Abel - because the passage continues as such: *"...and she gave birth to Cain...2 Later she gave birth to his brother and <u>named him Abel.</u>"*

One consummation act produced two births.

---

[1] I like to think the name Eve is a historical marker to memorialize when their disobedience was discovered (i.e., "When the cool evening breezes were blowing...").

A Question of Paternity

Genesis 4:25 gives us the same vague account regarding the birth of Seth.

> "Adam had sexual relations with his wife <u>again</u>, and she gave birth to another son. <u>She named him</u> Seth."

Nevertheless, while the traditional presumption is that "formed" man (Adam) fathered Cain and Abel, the scriptures do not support this traditional presumption. However, what is supported is that "formed" man (Adam) never procreated with the (Wo)man/Eve.

Even though today's renderings of the scriptures have topical divisions, what at first appears to be intentional vagueness gives rise to an interesting writing style. Further on the genealogy of each "Adam" is introduced and what emerges in the written account of the descendants is a pattern that documents the establishment of the progeny and the subsequent death of the progenitor.

Yet, in the case of the lineage of Cain, Abel, and, in particular Seth, the progenitors are not pronounced to be deceased:

> 5:1 This is the book of the generations of Adam. In the day that God created man, in the likeness of God made he him; 5:2 male and female created he them; and blessed them, and called their name Adam, in the day when they were created.
>
> KJV

But in the case of "formed" man (Adam), the pattern changes in a manner whereby we may affirmatively conclude "formed" man (Adam) was never pronounced to be the father of a child through a sexual relationship with the (Wo)man / Eve.

Paramours

Moreover, when "formed" man (Adam) is assigned *putative* paternity *the language never says "this" Adam had sexual relations with his wife, Eve.* It says only:

> 5:3 "When Adam was 130 years old, he became the father of a son who was just like him - in his very image. <u>He named his son</u> Seth...
>
> 5:4 **Adam live 930 years, and then he died."**

"Formed" man's (Adam) death fulfilled the *Creator's* punishment imputed to him for eating fruit from the tree of the knowledge of good and evil: Genesis 2:17 ("...you are sure to die.") and Genesis 3:19 ("For you were made from dust, and to dust you will return.").

"Formed" man (Adam) became the father of one named son, **Seth, <u>who was named by his father</u>** (i.e., "formed" man (Adam))[2].

"Created" man (Adam) begot three named sons Cain, Abel, and **Seth <u>who were named by their mother</u>**.

Yes! The Serpent/Revealer/Adam is the father of Cain, Abel, and Seth.

So, was Cain's murder of Abel only the beginning of the enmity between the "formed" and the "created"? Or was it exacerbated with the birth of the Seth who was a product of a relationship between the "formed" man and the "created" female?

---

[2] Two Adams; two Seths. To this point, as a matter of practice, everything named was done by Adam (formed man). See also, Luke 1: 57-66.

4:26 And to Seth, to him also there was born a son, and he called his name Enos: then began men to call upon
The Name of the LORD.

Genesis (KJV)

THE ANTITHESIS

8:5 For though there be that are called gods
whether in heaven or in earth, as
There Are Gods Many, and Lords Many.

1 Corinthians (KJV)

THE RUSE

THE ANTITHESIS

And ... Then

¹⁶ Know ye not, that to whom ye yield yourselves servants to obey, his servants ye are to whom ye obey; whether of sin unto death, or of obedience unto righteousness?

Romans (KJV

:

The Reading

Genesis 6:

"¹ Then the people began to multiply on the earth, and daughters were born to them. ² The sons of God saw the beautiful women and took any they wanted as their wives.

³ Then the LORD said, "My Spirit will not put up with *humans* for such a long time, for they are only mortal flesh. In the future, **their normal lifespan will be no more than 120 years.**

⁴ In these days, and for some time after, giant Nephilites lived on the earth, for whenever the sons of **God** had intercourse with women, they gave birth to children who became heroes and famous warriors of ancient times.

⁵ So the **LORD** observed the extent of *human* wickedness on the earth, and he saw that everything they thought or imagined was consistently and totally evil.

⁶ So the **LORD** was sorry he had ever **made them** and put them on earth. It broke his heart.

⁷ And the **LORD** said, "I will wipe this *human race* I have created from the face of the earth. Yes, and I will destroy every living thing— all the people, the large animals, the smalls animals that scurry along the ground, and even the birds of the sky. I am sorry I ever made them."

THE ANTITHESIS

Favor

⁸ But Noah found favor with the **LORD.**

⁹ This is the account of Noah and his family. Noah was a righteous man, the only blameless person living on earth at the time, and he walked in close fellowship with **GOD.** ¹⁰ Noah was the father of three sons: Shem, Ham, and Japheth.

¹¹ Now **GOD** saw that the earth had become corrupt and was filled with violence. ¹² **GOD** observed all this corruption in the world, for everyone on earth was corrupt. ¹³ So **GOD** said to Noah, "I have decided to destroy all living creatures, for they have filled the earth with violence. Yes, I will wipe them all out along with the earth!"

¹⁴ "Build a boat... ¹⁷ Look! I am about to cover the earth with a ***flood that will destroy every living thing that breathes. Everything on earth will die.***

¹⁸ But I will confirm my covenant with you. So, enter the boat— you and your wife and your sons and their wives.

¹⁹ **Bring a pair of every kind of animal**— a male and a female - into the boat with you to keep them alive during the flood.

²⁰ **Pairs of every kind of bird**, and every kind of animal, and every kind of small animal that scurries along the ground, will come with you to be kept alive.

²¹ And be sure to take on board enough food for your family and for all the animals."

²² So Noah did everything exactly as **GOD** had commanded him.

Or did he?

The Reading

Genesis 7:

[1] When everything was ready, the **LORD** said to Noah, "Go into the boat with all your family, for among all the people of the earth, I can see that <u>you alone are righteous</u>.

[2] **Take with you seven pairs**— male and female— of each animal I have approved for eating and for sacrifice and take one pair of each of the others.

[3] Also **take seven pairs of every kind of bird**. There must be a male and female in each pair to ensure that all <u>life will survive on the earth after the flood</u>.

[4] **Seven days from now** I will make the rains pour down on the earth. And it will rain for forty days and forty nights, until I have *wiped from the earth <u>all living things I have created</u>.*"

[5] So Noah did everything as the **LORD** commanded him.

[6] **Noah was 600 years old** when the flood covered the earth. [7] He went on board the boat to escape the flood - <u>he and his wife and his sons and their wives</u>.

THE ANTITHESIS

The Digression

8 With them were all the various kinds of animals - those approved for eating and for sacrifice and those that were not - along with all the birds and small animals that scurry along the ground. 9 They entered the boat in pairs, male and female, just as God had commanded Noah. 10 After seven days, the waters of the flood came and covered the earth... 21 All the living things on earth died... 22 Everything that had breath and lived on dry land died... All were destroyed. **The only people who survived were Noah and those with him in the boat.** 24 And the flood waters covered the earth for 150 days.

Genesis 7

"The only people who survived were Noah and those with him in the boat" is not as specific as "he and his wife and sons and their wives" – as declared in Genesis 7:7 ... implying the possibility of stowaways?

Just as an interesting segue, I would just introduce a little food-for-thought.

> 6:4 "In those days, and for some time after, giant Nephilites lived on the earth..."

In Genesis 6:4, the Nephilims are brought into the discussion for a cameo. The etymology of the term *nephilim,* according to the *Young's Analytical Concordance to the Bible*, refers to "fallen one."

> 14:12 How art thou fallen from heaven, O Lucifer, son of the morning! how art thou cut down to the ground, which didst weaken the nations!

Isaiah

With that said we also discover that the Nephilims - sons of Anak who is the son of Arba (i.e., *strength of Baal*) - survived the flood, as well.

The Ordinance

Genesis 8:

[20] Then Noah built an altar to the LORD, and there he sacrificed as burnt offerings the animals and birds that had been approved for that purpose. [21] And the LORD was pleased with the aroma of the sacrifice...

Genesis 9:

Then God blessed Noah and his sons and told them to be fruitful and multiply. Fill the earth. [2] All the animals of the earth, all the birds of the sky, all the small animals that scurry along the ground, and all the fish in the sea will look on you with great fear and terror. I have placed them in your power. [3] I have given them to you for food, just as I have given you grain and vegetables. [4] But you must never eat any meat that still has the lifeblood in it.

[5] "And I will require the blood of anyone who takes another person's life. If a wild animal kills a person, it must die. And anyone who murders a fellow human must die. [6] If anyone takes a human life, that person's life will also be taken by human hands. For God made human beings ***in his own image***..."

THE BEGINNING OF THE END

The Language

I would like to start this part of the discussion with a "flashback" to the accounts of Genesis 1 through Genesis 5.

Throughout the account of creation in Genesis 1 the "Creator" is referred to as God. Example:

> 1:27 "So God created human beings in his own image."

Once we proceed beyond the account of creation (Genesis 2:4), the referent changes to the LORD God. Example:

> 2:7 "Then the LORD God formed the man from the dust of the ground... 2:8 then the LORD God planted a garden in Eden... and there he placed the man he had made."

In Genesis 3, we begin to notice that when accounts of creation are referenced the term God is used and when other accounts are referenced the term LORD God is used. Example:

> 3:1 "The serpent was the shrewdest of <u>all the wild animals the LORD God had made</u>. One day he asked the woman, "<u>Did God really say you must not eat</u> the fruit from any of the trees in the garden?"

> 3:8 When the cool evening breezes were blowing, the man and his wife heard <u>the LORD God walking about</u> in the garden."

Thus, clearly LORD and God give respect to different offices of position and authority ... 1) God being a superhuman being or spirit worshipped as having power over nature and/or human forces; 2) LORD being someone or something having authority or *influence* by hereditary right or preeminence and to whom service and obedience are due.

Upon being expelled from the Garden of Eden, it became self-evident that the "Creator" was emphatic about wanting "formed" man (Adam) and the (Wo)man/Eve to die:

> 3:22 "Behold the man is become as one of us... and lest he put forth his hand, and take also of the tree of life, and eat, and live forever;"

> 3:24 "So he drove out the man: and he placed at the east of the garden of Eden cherubim, and a flaming sword which turned every way, to keep the way of the tree of life."
>
> KJV

However, in Genesis 4, not only does the term LORD become the prevalent referent, but the fate of the human race takes an unintended turn. Example:

> 4:3 "When it was time for the harvest, Cain presented some of his crops as a gift (offering) to the LORD...

> 4:15 Then the LORD put a mark on Cain to warn anyone who might want to kill him..."

Thus, at this point, we have at least two opposing divinities - one with a vested interest in the demise of man and the other with a vested interest in man's continued existence.

> 4:26 ... **At that time people first began to worship <u>the LORD</u> by name**.

People began to worship <u>the LORD</u> by name. By what name? And why did people not begin to worship God?

Immaculate Conception(s)

Although "formed" man (Adam) and the (Wo)man/Eve experienced a quite different form of existence within the Garden, neither was embodied (*imprisoned*) in animal flesh until the expulsion:

> 3:21 And the LORD God made clothing from animal skins for Adam and his wife.
>
> Genesis

The (Wo)man/Eve was the progenitrix who incubated the animating spirit of the "Creator"; thus, offering the sons of God the best of both worlds (the coupling of celestial and mundane knowledge packaged in earthly beauty).

The sons of God (descendants of *"created"* male and female), however, were never specimens embodied in flesh, nevertheless, they were able to sire offspring with descendants of the (Wo)man/Eve.

> 6:1 "Then the people began to multiply on the earth, and daughters were born to them.
>
> 6:2 The sons of God saw the beautiful women, took any they wanted as their wives.
>
> 6:4 In those days... for whenever **the sons of God had intercourse with women,** they gave birth to children who became heroes and famous warriors of ancient times."

Since the sons of "God" did not have physical bodies the birth of Jesus (the Christ) was not the first and only immaculate conception recorded.

THE ANTITHESIS

It would be thematically unconscionable to fathom the same "God" that, allegedly, condemned this practice in Genesis 6 would (Himself) later perform the exact same prohibited act with the Virgin Mary:

1:18   This is how Jesus the Messiah was born. His mother, Mary, was engaged to be married to Joseph. But before the marriage took place, **while she was still a virgin,** she became **pregnant through the power of the Holy Spirit.**

1:19   Joseph, her fiancé, was a good man and did not want to disgrace her publicly... 1:20 As he considered this, an angel of the LORD appeared to him in a dream, "Joseph, son of David," the angel said, "do not be afraid to take Mary as your wife. For the child within her was conceived by the Holy Spirit.

1:24   When Joseph woke up, he did as the angel of the LORD commanded and took Mary as his wife.

Matthew

Which compels one to broach the question: "Is the God of Genesis 1-6 the same God of Matthew.

Thus, I am no more of the consensus that the immaculate conceptions of Genesis 6 neither rendered man anymore wicked than the epithet *serpent* that was *projected* upon "created" man (Adam) for revealing truth to the (wo)man about the enlightening properties of the fruit from the tree of knowledge of good and evil. Besides, the "created" male and female were commanded to ***"[b]e fruitful and multiply."***

Nevertheless, the developing pattern here depicts the label of "evil" as being attributed to any act deemed *not satisfactory* to the "Creator."

A Walk with God

^{6:7} I will wipe this *human race* I have created from the face of the earth... I am sorry I ever made them."

Psychologists use the term "projection" as an unconscious self-defense mechanism characterized by unconsciously attributing one's own issues onto someone else or something else...

In this case the acts of the sons of God thwarted the death sentence imputed to *"formed"* man (Adam) and Eve by the LORD God. Nothing seemed to be going His way; the *humans* shared divine knowledge with the *mundane* and now His remaining progeny have allied with *outcasts* to prolong the carrying out of the imposed sentence of death to *"formed"* man and his wife.

Therefore, since the sons of God who did not possess bodies of mortal flesh intervened in the natural course of events, **He resolved to destroy the human race** ... because they and their demigod/demigoddess off-spring were born into a body of mortal flesh (a carnal prison/sin).

We are told that Noah was a righteous man, the only blameless person living on earth at the time, and *he walked in close fellowship with God.*

In an earlier account, we find another individual who lived in close fellowship with God - Enoch. However, Enoch ... *walking in close fellowship with God* one day disappeared - because "God" took him.

Then if Noah was the only *blameless person living on earth at the time,* why did God not take Noah with Him, as well?

THE ANTITHESIS

A Spiritual Conspiracy

6:8 But Noah found favor with the L ORD.

As far as that is concerned, then, why was Noah's family allowed to escape the pending flood? By implication, they were as wicked as the others who were slated for destruction.

Thus, the question remains... with whom did Noah find favor?

With that said what becomes apparent during the rest of this discourse is the disparity with whom Noah is obeying.

(a) The **L ORD** was sorry He had ever made them and put them on the earth: thus, He said:

> 6:7 "I will wipe **this *human race* I have created** from the face of the earth. Yes, and I will destroy every living thing - all the people, the large animals, the small animals that scurry along the ground, and <u>even the birds of the sky</u>. I am sorry I ever made them."

This attitude is attributable to the acts of the "Creator" in Genesis 1, 2, and 3:

> 1:27 "So God *created human beings* in his own image."
> 2:27 "Then the L ORD God *formed the man from the dust of the ground.*"
> 3:8 "When the cool evening breezes were blowing, the man and his wife heard <u>the L ORD God walking about</u> in the garden."

Wherefore, at this point, we see that the term L ORD is being used as a referent for a divinity that has **a vested interest in the *destruction of the human race.***

(b) Then "God" said:

> 6:3 "I have decided to destroy <u>all living creatures</u>, for they have filled the earth with violence. Yes<u>, I will wipe them out along with the earth</u>!

> 6:14 **"Build a large boat**... 17 Look! <u>I am about to cover the earth with a flood</u>...

> 6:18 But I will confirm my covenant with you. So, enter the boat - <u>you and your wife and your sons and their wives</u>.

Now this referent never claims to have created anything that He plans to destroy.

What is particularly interesting is that this referent directs Noah to *build a boat* and to *bring a pair* of every kind of animal with him to keep them alive during the flood:

> 6:19 **Bring a pair of every kind of animal** - a male and a female - into the boat with you to keep them alive during the flood...

> 6:21 And be sure to **take on board enough food for your family and for all the animals."**

> 6:22 So <u>Noah did everything exactly as</u> **God** had commanded him.

Thus, for now and in name only, the "Creator" *God* of Genesis 1 - 3 *has been supplanted* by a divinity who has a vested interest in the continued existence of the human race, which is an attitude attributable to the LORD of Genesis 4:

> 4:15 Then the LORD put a mark on Cain to **warn anyone who might want to kill him..."**

Amicus Curiae

(c) Yet, when we get to Genesis 7, we find Noah received a subsequent set of instructions, which at face value makes the "LORD" / "God" - if considered to be the same divinity - appear rather divisive or at the very least ... indecisive:

> 7:2 **Take with you seven pairs** - male and female - of *each animal I have approved for eating and for sacrifice* and take <u>one pair of each of the others.</u>

> 7:3 Also **take seven pairs of every kind of bird**. There must be a male and a female in each pair to ensure that all life will survive on the earth after the flood.

> 7:5 So <u>Noah did everything as the **LORD**</u> commanded him.

Upon further contemplation we notice this divinity neither claims to have created anything on earth nor does this divinity make any statements with regards to how to create the façade of a destruction that wipes away earth and all its inhabitants.

This divinity, like the other, expresses a vested interest in the continued existence of the *human race* in addition to the institution of the practice of sacrifice and the continued availability of a sacrifice." "Take with you <u>seven pairs</u>... of each animal I have <u>approved for sacrifice</u> and take <u>one pair of each of the others.</u>"

A Thirst for Blood

Wait! The "Creator" God of Genesis 1-3 did not institute sacrifice nor the eating of animal flesh for sustenance:

> 1:29 Then God said, "Look! <u>I have given you every seed-bearing plant throughout the earth and all the fruit trees for your food.</u>
>
> 1:30 And <u>I have given every green plant as food for all the wild animals,</u> the birds in the sky, and the small animals that scurry along the ground - everything that has life."

Neither does any subsequent language indicate that the LORD of Genesis 4 require man to eat animal flesh for sustenance nor the institution of sacrifice:

> 4:2 When they grew up, Abel became a shepherd, while Cain cultivated the ground.
>
> 4:3 When it was time for harvest, <u>Cain presented</u> some of his crops as <u>a gift to the LORD</u>.
>
> 4:4 <u>Abel also brought a gift</u> - the best of the firstborn lambs from his flock. The LORD accepted Abel and his gift,
>
> 4:5 but he did not accept Cain and his gift. This made Cain very angry, and he looked dejected.

So, who is having <u>this</u> *ex-parte* communication with Noah?

THE ANTITHESIS

The Sorority

During the creation account of Genesis 1, "God" created ... in his own image ... male and female. Subsequently, in Genesis 2, the LORD God ... took out one of the man's ribs ... [and] made a help meet for him. "Formed" man called her (wo)man. Thus, there was female and (wo)man.

Like there were two men – Adam ... one created, the other formed. Likewise, the men had female counterparts ... one created, the other formed.

Along with created man (Adam) the created female received the *Creator's* blessing to "*be fruitful and multiply.*" To the contrary, formed man (Adam) and the (wo)man formed from the man's own rib did not receive that same blessing. Therefore, together, they were unable to procreate.

Nevertheless, as the scriptures will demonstrate, the absence of that blessing did not negate formed man (Adam) and his (wo)man the ability to be fruitful and multiply. They just were unable to do so with each other... they did not bear the inherent animating spirit bestowed upon the male and female.

The first evidence the scripture gives us into (wo)man's ability to reproduce is foreshadowed in Genesis 3: "I will cause hostility between ... your offspring and her offspring ... and in pain will you give birth."

This foreshadowing came to fruition in Genesis 4: "Now Adam had sexual relations with his wife, Eve, and she became pregnant ..."

In Genesis 5 we are told Adam (formed man) was 130-years old when he became the father of a son who was just like him – in his very image. Adam (formed man) named his son Seth. The same name that Eve named her third son with Adam (created man).

Within the Jewish tradition another female, Lilith, existed during this period. Because I have no inspired knowledge, nor understanding of Lilith I will not expound upon her role – as expressed within Jewish theology. For this purpose, she is mentioned only to demonstrate that this author is not the only student submitting scriptural evidence to substantiate this assertion.

This author proposes Adam's (formed man's) son, Seth, was sired with the created female. Thus, this Seth was a demigod; just like the offspring of Eve with Adam (created man). They both were grafted into the family of *human beings*.

Earlier the question was broached [The Imposition] as part of her punishment (wo)man was to experience pain in birth. Does that mean (wo)man had given birth before – without pain. The answer is no. However, (wo)man witnessed childbirth without the mother experiencing pain. This pleasure she/(wo)man would not come to know, personally.

THE ANTITHESIS

Reflections

We have covered quite a few items and here is where we summarize our stance:

1) Earth was already in existence prior to the creation account of Genesis 1 et seq.

2) There is no issue with the chronological references to "created" man (Adam) of Genesis 1:27 and "formed" man (Adam) of Genesis 2:7. There were two men called "Adam" just as there were two Seths.

3) Likewise, there are two females involved in this saga – the "created" female and Eve, the (wo)man made from the "formed" man.

4) The Serpent/Adam never lied nor deceived the (Wo)man/Eve. The only actor within this epic that was not so forthcoming with the truth was the "Creator."

5) Prior to Genesis 3:21, neither "Adam" (created nor formed) nor the (wo)man/Eve had a fleshy covering over their bodies as traditionally viewed. Therefore, the nakedness for which they were ashamed cannot be properly understood as they [(wo)man and "formed" man (Adam)] desired to cover their genitalia.

6) Sin is not an act; it was the result of an act. The result was for (Wo)man/Eve and "formed" man (Adam) to have their innate bodies *imprisoned* in animal skins. Wherefore, now all humans are born into sin (that fleshy covering [husk] where you are committed to carry out a divine death sentence).

About the Author

In 1987 I was called into the ministry. For two years *I* – as many called into this vocation – *ran from my calling*. For two years I endured a spiritual chastisement that, at times, caused me to believe I was losing my mind. I saw, heard, and understood things as others did not. I made my life more perplexing than necessary (Jonah 1).

Once I accepted *my calling*, I walked the precipice of a *brotherhood* comprised of preachers, pastors, ministers, etc. Who do I emulate? However, I was not of the same fabric that made the garment of the old guard.

My defining moment came while conversing with a diminutive giant who I highly respected. During that night service, I remained in the pastorate with him, and he uttered the most powerful words any member of the *brotherhood* had ever said to me prior: "Let your calling mold you." That night I felt like Amos:

> "I'm not a professional prophet, and I was never trained to be one … But the Lord … told me, 'Go and prophesy to my people…'" (7:14,15)

Through various interactions in many venues and the use of storied platforms, I realized the path to fulfill my "commission" lies within the use of one of the oldest forms known to civilization … writing.

Thus, for a time such as this, I have postured myself to carry out my commission and, hopefully, assist you in finding your path, realize your niche, and equip you to fulfill your great commission.

Also by the Author

Additional titles on the horizon to look for:

Hegemony

An exposé of how societal laws and norms established by political and financial influencers affect the lives of common citizens. Based on a true story, see how one citizen adapted and evolved amidst the matrix of life's ever changing environmental factors.

From Out of Nazareth

Stars, celebrities, and the like are not viewed by their children, siblings, and childhood friends as they are viewed and treated by those outside their intimate circles. Leaning upon scriptures, this book steps inside an intimate circle outside of public life and looks at Jesus in a, respectful, yet different light.

...Think On These Things.

The prequel to *The Antithesis* addresses the power dynamics we self-attach to a name as opposed to the assets, attributes, and/or quality of the individual entity living within the legacy of an assigned office.